There are all those early memories;
one cannot get another set. . . .

—Willa Cather

CRACKED CORN AND SNOW ICE CREAM

A FAMILY ALMANAC

by NANCY WILLARD

Illustrations by

JANE DYER

HARCOURT BRACE & COMPANY

San Diego   New York   London

A special thanks to
JULIE FREEMAN,
who drove us around Iowa and was the first
to suggest that these stories should be written down.
She planted the seed.

And thank you to
DIANE D'ANDRADE,
who nurtured it along,
and kept it watered and weeded.

—J. D. *and* N. W.

Text copyright © 1997 by Nancy Willard
Illustrations copyright © 1997 by Jane Dyer

Requests for permission to make copies of any part of the work should
be mailed to: Permissions Department, Harcourt Brace & Company,
6277 Sea Harbor Drive, Orlando, Florida 32887-6777.

Library of Congress Cataloging-in-Publication Data
Willard, Nancy.
Cracked corn and snow ice cream: a family almanac/Nancy Willard;
illustrated by Jane Dyer.
p. cm.
Summary: Provides rural information ("Do not disturb your bees in
cold weather") and family voices for each month of the year.
ISBN 0-15-227250-X
1. Almanacs, Children's. [1. Almanacs.] I. Dyer, Jane, ill. II. Title.
AY81.J8W55 1997
031.02—dc20 96-4198

B D F G E C

The illustrations in this book were done in Winsor and Newton
watercolors on Arches 140 lb. hot press watercolor paper.
The display type was hand-lettered by Jane Dyer.
The text type was set in Caslon 540 and Caslon No. 3.
Color separations by Bright Arts, Ltd., Singapore
Printed and bound by Tien Wah Press, Singapore
This book was printed on totally chlorine-free Nymolla Matte Art paper.
Production supervision by Stanley Redfern and Ginger Boyer
Designed by Jane Dyer, Camilla Filancia, and Barry Age

Printed in Singapore

JANUARY ❄ has 31 days

When icicles hang by the wall,
And Dick the shepherd blows his nail,
And Tom bears logs into the hall,
And milk comes frozen home in pail,
When blood is nipped, and ways be foul,
Then nightly sings the staring owl,
Tu-whit,
tu-who, a merry note,
While greasy Joan doth keel the pot.

William Shakespeare
LOVE'S LABOUR'S LOST

DATES AND FESTIVALS

1 *New Year's Day*

6 **Epiphany** Three Kings' Day

13 *Charlotte Ray,* first African American woman lawyer, is born, 1850.

15 **Martin Luther King Jr.,** civil rights leader and winner of the Nobel Peace Prize, is born, 1929.

17 **Benjamin Franklin** is born, 1706.

19 *Robert E. Lee,* general in chief of the Confederate armies during the Civil War, is born, 1807.

Edgar Allan Poe, writer, is born, 1807.

27 *Wolfgang Amadeus Mozart,* composer, is born, 1756.

VARIABLE FEAST DAYS AND HOLIDAYS

CHINESE NEW YEAR ◆ Dates set by the phases of the moon.

◆ **PLOW SUNDAY** ◆
In medieval England the blessing of the plows occurred on the Sunday after Epiphany.

THE NEXT DAY MEN WOULD DECK A PLOW WITH RIBBONS & DRAG IT FROM FARMHOUSE TO FARMHOUSE SHOUTING, "GOD SPEED THE PLOW." IF THE HOUSEHOLDER DID NOT GIVE THEM MONEY, THEY MIGHT PLOW UP HIS FRONT YARD.

Take down Christmas decorations by January 6 (Twelfth Night). It's thought that to leave them up longer will bring bad luck.

FOR GOOD LUCK: Turn your apron over when you see the new moon.

JANUARY ❄ the first month

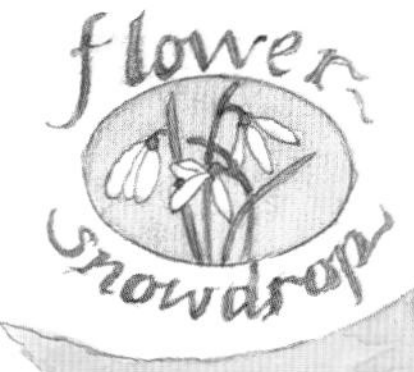

flower
Snowdrop

FARMER'S CALENDAR

BIRTHSTONE
• garnet
FOR CONSTANCY

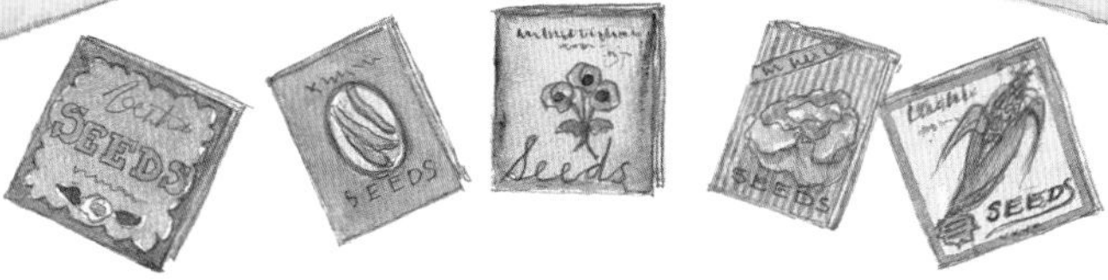

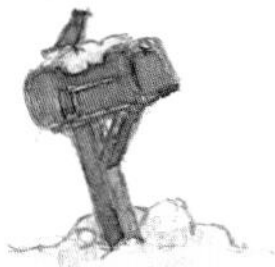

When seed catalogs appear in your mailbox, it's time to plan your garden; order your seeds now.

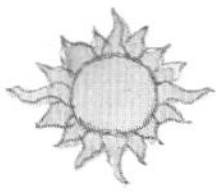

Give your cows the freedom of a sunny yard for several hours each day.

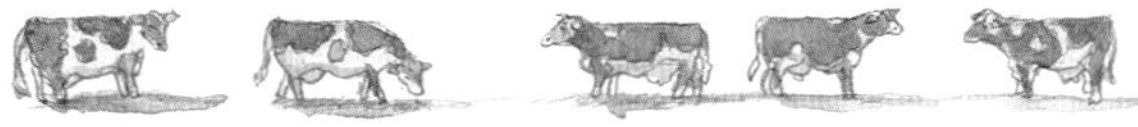

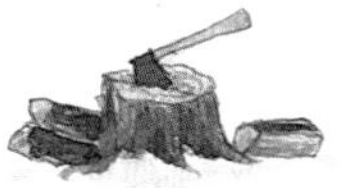

Prune your grapevines, cut your firewood, and cut ice to store for use in summer. Pack and cover your ice with straw or sawdust.

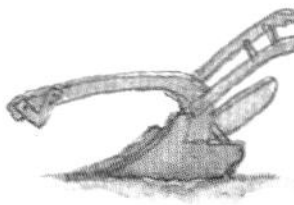

Check all machines, tools, and harnesses, and repair them.

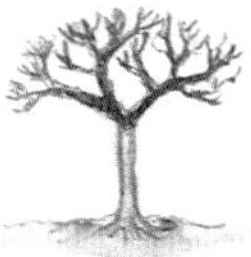

Protect your young trees against sunscald. Whitewash the trunk up to the lowest branch. SNOW INCREASES THE GLARE OF THE SUN, WHICH HEATS UP THE BARK.

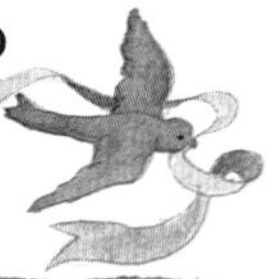

TEN MOST POPULAR VEGETABLES GROWN BY GARDENERS

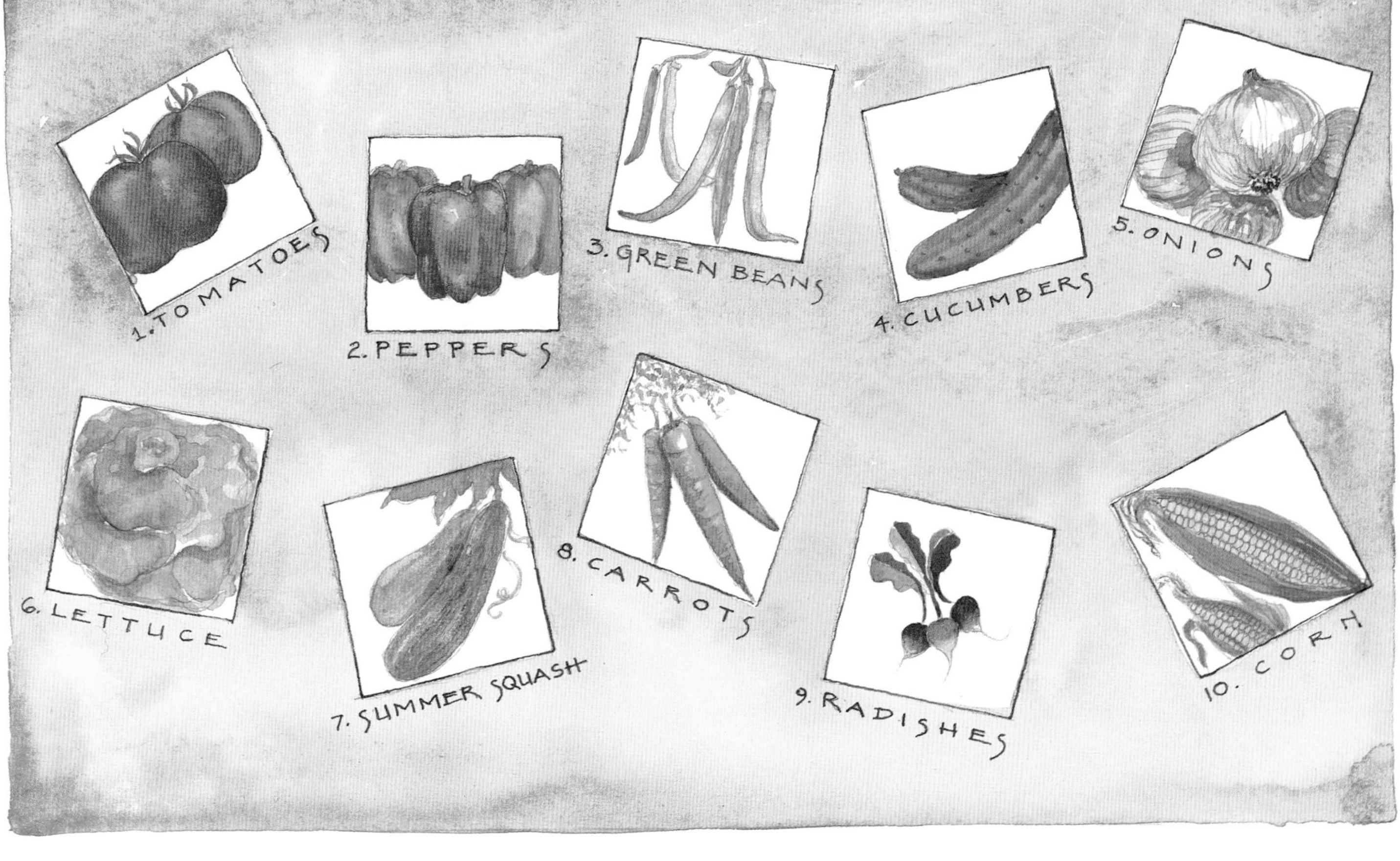

1. TOMATOES
2. PEPPERS
3. GREEN BEANS
4. CUCUMBERS
5. ONIONS
6. LETTUCE
7. SUMMER SQUASH
8. CARROTS
9. RADISHES
10. CORN

JANUARY

WORTH KNOWING

❄ For frostbitten feet: Keep your feet in warm, not hot, water and let them thaw slowly. Too much heat will cause further injury.

❄ If you soak your clothespins in strong salt brine, they will not freeze to the clothesline. One soaking should last the winter.

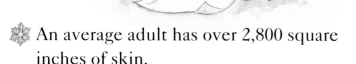

❄ An average adult has over 2,800 square inches of skin.

❄ On January 28, 1887, snowflakes "larger than milkpans," fifteen inches across and eight inches thick, were reported falling near Fort Keogh, Montana.

❄ "Happy Birthday to You" was written by the Hill sisters, Patty Smith, Mildred, and Jessica, in 1893.

WORTH COOKING

Snow Ice Cream

1 can evaporated milk
1/2 cup sugar
1 tsp. vanilla
large amount of freshly fallen snow

Mix milk and sugar in large bowl until sugar is dissolved. Then add vanilla. Stir in fresh snow. (Add just as much snow as it needs to look and taste like vanilla ice cream.) Pour maple syrup or chocolate sauce over the top if you like. Eat it before it melts.

COW FACTS

• How many cows fit in an average classroom? *33*

• How many glasses of water a day does a cow drink? *Between 480 and 640 glasses. Cows drink between 30 and 40 gallons of water a day.*

• Milking by hand: There are 340 squirts in one gallon of milk.

• A cow has one stomach with four parts. It can take as long as four days for a cow to digest a feeding of hay.

THE VOICES

In winter I played in the attic. I had a cardboard box that I made into a house. I wallpapered it and cut furniture out of a Sears catalog.

—ALBERTA REIMER

THE VOICES

In the winter there was lots of snow. Sometimes we couldn't even stay on the road. We'd have to ride over to the fences in the fields, to wherever the snow would hold us. Cows and horses and chickens—all of us traveled there.

We didn't use the buggy. We used a sleigh. My sister would sit in between my mother and father, and I would sit on a footstool. There was a special stone my mother heated in the oven to keep our feet warm. She wrapped it in a cloth so it wouldn't burn our boots. I think it was called "soapstone."

—LORETTA KORFHAGE

here were times the air never got warmed up in the house.

—HAROLD WIEDOW

I was born in that house down there. It was a coach house at one time. The stagecoach used to come by here, and they'd change the horses at that house.

—ALTON WOLF

 didn't have a birth certificate. The doctor didn't give me one because he didn't think I'd live. My grandmother wrapped me up in blankets and laid me in a box on the hot water reservoir of our woodstove.

I had a little tin doll, and her head was about two inches around, and when I asked my father how big I was, he said, "When you were born, you were no bigger than this tin-headed doll." I cried and cried to think I was as small as that.

—L. K.

When I was a baby, my mother told my father that she had to have a carriage because I was too heavy to carry. My father said they cost ten dollars, and that was too much, but finally gave in. It had a pink satin parasol, but we never used it. This picture was taken in the garden.

—A. R.

e used kerosene for the lamps. We had to brush the chimneys of the lamps each day, or they'd smoke up. It was a terrible job to clean them—they'd get so black. We had the toilet outside.

—L. K.

FEBRUARY

~ has 28 days

except in Leap Year, when it has 29

The sun's feet give off
a faint red glow
the rimefrost on the cassia branches
doesn't melt

now and then a warm breeze
tries to drive winter off
as the days grow longer
and the long nights end.

Li Ho

DATES AND FESTIVALS

2 Groundhog Day. If the groundhog sees his shadow, we'll have six more weeks of winter.

3 St. Blasius's Day. St. Blasius was a bishop and a doctor skilled at healing both people and animals.

THE SERVICE FOR THE **BLESSING OF THE THROATS** TAKES PLACE ON THIS DAY

Elizabeth Blackwell, the first woman medical doctor in the United States, is born, 1821.

9 St. Apollonia's Day. St. Apollonia is the patron saint of those who suffer from toothache. 🦷

The Weather Bureau is founded, 1870.

11 Thomas Edison is born, 1847. 💡

12 Abraham Lincoln is born, 1809.

14 Valentine's Day ♥ *According to legend, St. Valentine is the patron saint of those who wish to marry & has the power to mend lover's quarrels.*

 The date *Frederick Douglass,* abolitionist and orator, chose for his birthday, 1817. The actual date is unknown.

15 Susan B. Anthony, leader in the movement to give women the right to vote, is born, 1820.

17 Alberta Reimer is born, 1916.

22 George Washington is born, 1732.

26 Sixteen Native American chiefs ask the U.S. government to let them stay on their ancestral lands in upper Michigan: *"We love the spot where our forefathers bones are laid, and we desire that our bones may rest beside theirs also."* 1855

During a snowstorm on February 13, 1853, on Mount Desert Island, Maine, purplish ball lightning startled residents when it entered their homes through windows and down chimneys.

FEBRUARY ❤ the second month

VARIABLE FEAST DAYS AND HOLIDAYS

• FAT TUESDAY *or* MARDI GRAS •

Also called Carnival and Shrove Tuesday, a day of feasting and merriment before the fast of Lent. The word "carnival" comes from the Latin; it means "farewell to meat." These holidays can also fall in March.

• ASH WEDNESDAY •

The seventh Wednesday before Easter, and the day following Fat Tuesday. Christians receive ashes on the forehead as a sign of penitence.

• PURIM •

A Jewish holiday on the 14th day of the month of Adar. It honors Queen Esther's success in persuading the Persian king to reverse his decision to destroy the Jews.

flower **primrose**

FARMER'S CALENDAR

BIRTHSTONE
amethyst
FOR
SINCERITY

Use the snow to haul timber home from the sawmill or woodlot.

 Brush the snow from your evergreens to keep their limbs from breaking.

 Now is the time to prune grapevines, apple trees, plum trees, and cherry trees.

If you want your hens to lay through the winter months, hang a head of cabbage in the laying house.

 Do not disturb your bees in cold weather.

 Winter evenings are a good time to make nesting boxes for birds. Make them from hollow limbs, tin cans, or gourds.

1. MAKE THE ENTRANCE 2" OR MORE FOR MARTINS, BUT NO MORE THAN 1½" FOR BLUEBIRDS OR SWALLOWS, 1" FOR WRENS.
2. CUT HOLES HIGH ENOUGH TO KEEP BABY BIRDS FROM FALLING OUT.
3. MAKE 3 HOLES ~ THE SIZE OF A PENCIL ~ IN THE BOTTOM TO ALLOW FOR DRAINAGE.

The birds will repay you by catching troublesome insects.

FEBRUARY

NAMED FOR FEBRUAR,
the Roman goddess of health and healing.

WORTH KNOWING

- Lumbermen harvesting timber for the king's masts in pre-Revolutionary times reported finding, in Maine and New Hampshire, great pines six feet thick and 250 feet tall.

- If you want to know what the weather will be, watch pinecones. They open in good weather and close when storms are on the way.

- Sharpen your scissors by passing the blades over a glass jar.

COW FACTS

- In one day a cow eats a total of 81 pounds of food: 20 pounds of grain, 12 pounds of hay, and 49 pounds of silage.

- In addition to the cow shed, the dairy farm has a building called a milking parlor.

- How much waste does a full-grown cow make in one day?
  5 gallons of urine and 90 to 100 pounds of manure

WORTH COOKING

Hard Times Pudding

1 cup molasses
1 cup cold water
1 cup chopped raisins
1 tsp. salt
1 tsp. baking soda

Add flour enough to give pudding the thickness of soft gingerbread. Steam for two hours in a pudding mold or pail. Eat it with sugar.

TO FIND YOUR TRUE LOVE

- *Walk around the block with your mouth full of water. If you don't swallow it, you'll be married within the year.*
- *Set a silent supper late at night, taking care to do everything backward. Keep perfectly silent. Take your seat backward and at the stroke of midnight you will see the face of your true love.*
- *Count fifty white horses as you see them, and a white mule. Your groom will be the first unmarried man you shake hands with afterward.*

BASIL IS AN IMPORTANT INGREDIENT IN LOVE POTIONS. IT ENCOURAGES LOVE AT FIRST SIGHT.

THE VOICES

The doctor came to the house and wanted to take my tonsils out. He got his knife out, and I ran out in my nightshirt, right through the snow, and climbed the apple tree and wouldn't come down.

—CLARK WIEDOW

THE VOICES

All the German people from this area came from Mecklenburg. Did you ever hear how Grossvater ran away and came to America? See, he and his buddy were going to be drafted into the kaiser's army. So these two boys went to Hamburg and looked for a ship that was sailing to America, but there wasn't one leaving right away. They had to wait. One afternoon around the corner came two of the kaiser's soldiers. Those boys thought they'd be taken for sure.

Now, the German women of that day wore very full skirts, and there was a woman setting on the corner. She hid those boys under her skirt till the soldiers went by.

Took them six weeks to cross, but they got here. —HAROLD WIEDOW

My father's folks came from an area around Poland. They spoke what they call low German. And my mother's folks came from Bavaria. My mother spoke about people dying aboard the ship and how they were thrown into the ocean. —LORETTA KORFHAGE

On rainy days my mother would open the Russian trunk that my grandparents had used when they came to this country. My mother used it for treasures. In a tray in the lid were a pair of my big sister's baby shoes. They always fascinated me. They were white leather with black tops, and they buttoned. —ALBERTA REIMER

My father was very particular about his horses. In cold weather he'd always take a blanket along to church and put the blanket over them so they wouldn't freeze.

Between the barn and the shed was quite a distance, and my father had a windbreak built there, which we'd close to keep the wind from howling. —L. K.

I think I was in third grade when I got to bring a friend home for my birthday. I chose Lee Esther. She lived in town. I remember her house had hardwood floors that were varnished. She came home with me and we sat in the dining room. My mother made scrambled eggs for us. —A. R.

One Sunday morning my mother tried to put a big chunk of wood into the woodstove so it would hold a long time. And she had quite a time getting it in. She pinched her finger on the stove. It was very painful. And while we were at church, she fainted. We took her to the doctor in the minister's sleigh. —L. K.

SPRING

Above (left): ALTON WOLF with his mother

Above: LORETTA KORFHAGE and sister, MILDRED

Middle (left): LORETTA and MILDRED

Middle (right): HAROLD WIEDOW

Bottom (left): LORETTA's confirmation

Bottom (right): ALTON with sister, HAZEL

ALBERTA REIMER's mother *(far right)* in Model T

ALBERTA's father *(third from right, standing)*

ALBERTA *(right)* with sister, DORA

ALBERTA's parents on their wedding day

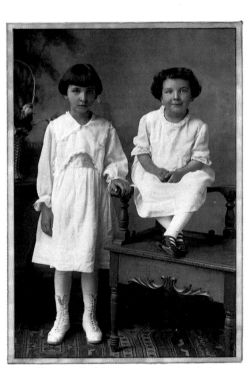

DORA *(left)*, ALBERTA *(right)*

ALBERTA's father

ALBERTA REIMER

Geese on ALBERTA's farm

MARCH ✦ has 31 days

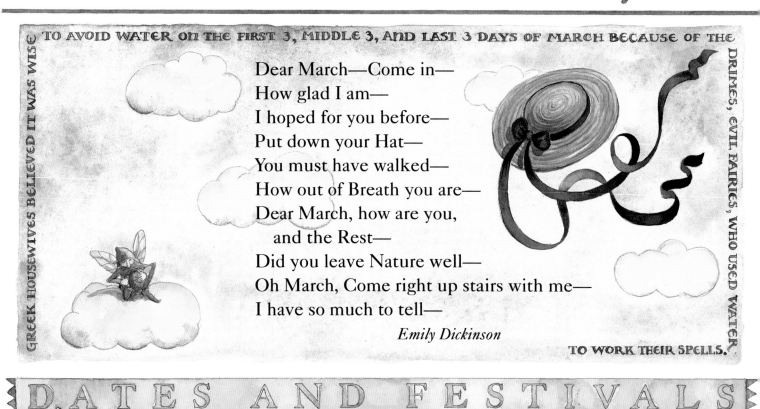

Dear March—Come in—
How glad I am—
I hoped for you before—
Put down your Hat—
You must have walked—
How out of Breath you are—
Dear March, how are you,
   and the Rest—
Did you leave Nature well—
Oh March, Come right up stairs with me—
I have so much to tell—

Emily Dickinson

DATES AND FESTIVALS

3 Postage stamps authorized for use, 1847.

15 In the ancient Roman calendar, Ides is the name for the fifteenth day of March, May, July, and October.

Julius Caesar is assassinated on the Ides of March, 44 B.C.

17 *St. Patrick's Day* ❧ ❧ ❧

19 Swallows return to San Juan Capistrano.

20 African American *Jan Ernst Matzeliger* receives a patent for a machine that stitches the top leather of a shoe to the sole, 1883.

production increases from 50 pairs of shoes a day to 700

21 Spring equinox, one of the two times in the year when day and night are equal

21 *Johann Sebastian Bach* is born, 1685.

23 *Fannie Farmer* is born, 1857.

She standardized cooking methods and published her first cookbook in 1896.

The Fannie Farmer Cookbook is still in print.

26 Poet *Robert Frost* is born, 1874.

28 *Nathaniel Briggs* patents the washing machine, 1797.

29 Niagara Falls are silenced for thirty hours by an ice jam at the neck of Lake Erie and the entrance to the Niagara River, 1848.

VARIABLE FEAST DAYS AND HOLIDAYS

EASTER· Since Easter falls on the first Sunday after the first full moon on or after the spring equinox, the possible dates range from March 22 to April 25.

PASSOVER· Eight days of celebration to commemorate the escape of the Jews from Egypt. Passover can also come in April.

Put up your nesting boxes. Choose a shady place beyond the reach of cats. If you set the boxes on fifteen-foot poles, the swallows and purple martins should be safe. The entrances should face south or west.

Sharpen all tools around the farm.

Hedge Shears · Grain Sickle · Pruning Shears · Corn Cutter · Scythe Grass Hook

Rake and burn dead leaves, old brush, and broken limbs in the woodlands around your barns and orchards. This will prevent fires during the dry season and will destroy the gypsy and brown-tail moths and other destructive insects.

THE CARE OF COWS

Keep your cow clean and wash the udders before you milk her. Carry the milk from the stable as soon as it is drawn, strain it, and cool it immediately. Do not expose it to bad odors and do not mix fresh, warm milk with milk that has been cooled. Do not excite the cow with loud talking.

🍁 MAPLE SUGARING 🍁

Wait for a sunny day, with a temperature of at least forty degrees, after a freezing night to tap your maple trees. Don't tap a maple tree that's less than ten inches in diameter.

🍁🍁🍁 TO MAKE THE SPIGOT:

Pick an elderberry bush stem and hollow it by pushing out the pith. In the south side of your tree, drill a hole, slanted slightly upward, 2 to 4 inches deep, and 3/8 to 3/4 of an inch wide. Tap the spigot into the hole, stopping just short of the full depth, and hang up your bucket. If you get your buckets up by ten in the morning, they should be full by suppertime.

🍁🍁 BOILING THE SAP TO MAKE MAPLE SYRUP:

"The sap must be closely watched while boiling. Just as soon as it begins to make eyes, it is taken off the fire and worked with a small paddle that looks like a canoe paddle. When we were children we used to watch for this stage in boiling, beg for a little sap on a piece of birch bark, drop it into the snow, and let it turn to gum."

—OJIBWA MAN

MARCH

NAMED FOR MARS,
the god of war and fertile fields

WORTH KNOWING

- Ireland is named for the warrior-queen Eire, who is said to have gathered an army against invading forces before 400 B.C.

- To stop a mouse hole, fill it with laundry soap.

- One of the best-known weather vanes in America is the giant grasshopper with green glass eyes hammered out of copper by Shem Drowne and placed on the roof of Faneuil Hall in Boston in the 1740s.

WORTH COOKING

Cottage Cheese

Heat very slowly 1 quart unpasteurized, naturally sour skim milk in a double boiler. Put it through a strainer lined with cheese-cloth and drain. Rinse with about 1 quart warm water and repeat rinsing two more times. Let drain until curd is free of the whey. Moisten with cream, and salt to taste.

Some useful birds~

BROWN CREEPER KINGLET SPARROW SCARLET TANAGER RED-EYED VIREO FLYCATCHER BLUEBIRD

Birds eat leafhoppers, grasshoppers, grubs, and other insect pests. Without the birds, a million leafhoppers in the pasture could eat as much grass as a cow.

NUTHATCH CATBIRD

DOWNY WOODPECKER TITMOUSE JUNCO WARBLER BARN SWALLOW

WEATHER WISE

The west wind is a good child who goes to bed at night.

THE VOICES

Well, there wasn't any supermarket. The store had barrels of sugar and flour and different things like that. I remember my mother bought some red flannel for Mildred and me, red with black dots in it. My cousin made us jumpers and trimmed them with black braid.

—LORETTA KORFHAGE

THE VOICES

My grandfather had a general merchandise store. It was called W. W. Johnson & Co. You could take your eggs in there and exchange them for cash or groceries.
—ALBERTA REIMER

Interior and exterior views of W.W. Johnson store.

 The mail came twice a day. The service was better than it is now. You could mail a letter for a penny. For twenty-five cents you could ride the mail steamer.
—L. K.

 My mother made her own cottage cheese. She put skim milk on the back of the stove. When it formed curds and whey, she drained it. I took it out to the ducklings to feed them, but I ate it on the way, it was so good.
—A. R.

 To get to school you had to be up by six o'clock, so you could finish your chores. Didn't matter if it was twenty below. We always had to milk the cows and clean the barn. We sold the cream. When we separated the cream, we dumped away the skim milk or fed it to the animals. And that skim milk was probably thicker than most milk you'd buy in the stores today.
—ALTON WOLF

 We had a small brown horse named Midge that my father drove to the creamery or when he took things to town. There were posts in front of the creamery where he would tie Midge. Mornings, my father went to the creamery to sell his milk. My sister and I rode to school with him. He had a number of customers who wanted to buy fresh milk from us. The women brought out their pails. And my father would dip into his cans and pour the milk out for them. He never separated the cream. The milk was richer, and he got more money for it.
—L. K.

 My mother would make new dresses for us—wool, with a satin or velvet panel. She would take the panel to a woman in town who would sew beaded flowers on it. The woman had patterns she made on brown paper and newspapers. Then my mother would insert the panel in the dress.
—A. R.

Oats, peas, beans, and barley grow,
Oats, peas, beans, and barley grow,
You nor I nor anyone knows
How oats, peas, beans, and barley grow.

First the farmer sows the seeds,
Then he stands and takes his ease,
He stamps his foot, and claps his hand,
And turns around to view the land.

DATES AND FESTIVALS

1 *April Fools' Day.* A day for the playing of practical jokes, observed in the United States since colonial times.

5 *Helen Keller* first understands the meaning of the word "water" when her teacher, Anne Sullivan, writes it in Helen's hand using the manual alphabet, 1887.

   Booker T. Washington, American educator and author of an autobiography, *Up from Slavery,* is born, 1856.

13 *Thomas Jefferson* is born, 1743.

15 *Bessie Smith,* blues singer, is born, 1894.

18 *Paul Revere's* ride, 1775.

18 San Francisco earthquake, 1906.

20 *Charles Albert Bender,* a Chippewa, begins his baseball career. He is the only Native American in the Baseball Hall of Fame.

23 *The Day of St. George,* the knight who is said to have killed a dragon so enormous that four oxcarts were needed to carry it away.

   William Shakespeare is born, 1564.

25 The first school for the deaf is started in Hartford, Connecticut, 1817.

26 *Sybil Ludington,* sixteen years old, rides from town to town in New York to warn colonists of a British raid on Danbury, Connecticut, 1777.

VARIABLE FEAST DAYS AND HOLIDAYS

PALM SUNDAY

The Sunday before Easter, celebrating Christ's triumphant entry into Jerusalem.

APRIL ❧ the fourth month

MAUNDY THURSDAY.

The day of the Last Supper. On this day the king of England, as penance, used to wash the feet of poor men, one for each year of his age.

GOOD FRIDAY, EASTER SUNDAY

These holidays can also come in March.

flower. DAISY

BIRTHSTONE *diamond* FOR INNOCENCE

FARMER'S CALENDAR

Sow wheat and rye as early as you can work the land.

During the first days of plowing, raise each horse's collar often to cool its shoulders.

Since crows and blackbirds are flying over the fields now, it's a good time to make a scarecrow.

To get an early start on your garden, plant lettuce, cauliflower, and cabbages in a cold frame.

If you have a damp cellar, you have a good place for growing mushrooms.

Dress your scarecrow in red, and birds will probably avoid it.

KRASHANKY **EASTER EGGS** PYSANKY

Ukrainian women decorate two kinds of eggs for Easter. Krashanky are hard-boiled eggs, brightly dyed one color. They were thought to have magic powers. Kept under a haystack, they would keep away strong winds. Buried under a beehive, they would bring a good harvest of honey. Farmers would roll a krashanka in green oats on St. George's Day and bury it in the fields to protect the crops.

Pysanky are blown eggs, dyed and elaborately decorated by using a stylus to draw the designs in beeswax. They were made not only for the priest, friends, and family, but also for the animals. Farmers rubbed them on animals to protect them.

Some say the first pysanky were brought by the birds, who were caught by a sudden freeze on their long journey south. Ukrainian peasants nursed the birds through the long winter. The birds rewarded them in the spring with a gift of decorated eggs.

WORTH KNOWING

- A slice of lemon or wet potato rubbed on your hands will help rid them of stains.

- A forgotten law in Owensburg, Kentucky: A woman cannot buy a new hat unless her husband tries it on first.

- The Dakota called the horse *sunka wakan*, "the mysterious dog."

- The smallest breed of horse is the Falabella, found in Argentina. It stands 12 to 40 inches tall and weighs less than 150 pounds.

- In Switzerland, it was the custom to plant a pear tree when a girl was born and an apple tree for a boy.

SUPERSTITIONS ABOUT GARDEN TOOLS:

- Never carry a spade indoors or lay down a rake with its teeth up.

- If you leave your hoe standing upright in the garden at the end of the day, you will not sleep that night.

- HERE ARE FIVE NAMES FOR THE SAME FLOWER: Irish daisy, timetable, blowball, fortune-teller, priest's crown.
  What's the flower?

ANSWER: Dandelion

WORTH COOKING

Dandelion Greens

To take the bitterness out of the young leaves, tie them together and cover them with a flower pot. This will blanch, or whiten, them.

When the leaves are well blanched, pick them, steam them, and eat them.

WEATHER WISE

- Rain before seven
  Clear before eleven.

- When clouds appear like rocks and towers,
  The earth's refreshed by frequent showers.

- If spiders are spinning new webs, look for fair weather.

- When dandelions stay closed till nine in the morning and snails climb up stalks of grass, rain is on the way.

- When clover, dandelions, tulips, or pimpernel close their petals, look for rain.

THE VOICES

We had ducks, geese, turkeys, chickens, and guineas. I carried water from the stock tank for them. We had cracked corn from the granary that we scattered over the farmyard for feed.
—ALBERTA REIMER

Alton Wolf feeding chickens with his mother.

THE VOICES

I'd have to collect the eggs from the chicken house. Usually my father would throw corn on the floor of the chicken house, and the chickens would jump out of their nests. While they were out, I'd gather the eggs. Some of the eggs were under hens just beginning to sit, and they didn't want to get out. I held a shingle over their heads so they wouldn't peck, and I'd grab them by the tail and throw them off the nest. Then I'd take the eggs.

Sometimes the wolves came after the chickens. —Loretta Korfhage

Dad was out in the field plowing. Mom was getting me ready to take the two horses to the field so I could follow him with the harrow. One of them was a driving horse, not a regular workhorse, like the other one, and she balked and reared up and pulled the workhorse back with her, right on top of the harrow. The harrow had big, sharp teeth. I was back there with the lines, trying to drive those horses out to my dad, and Mom grabbed me and pulled me through the barn door just as the horse and harrow and seemed like everything else piled up right in front of the barn door. While they were rolling, the teeth on the harrow opened up a big hole in that horse and tore the intestines out. They were just hanging on the ground.

—Harold Wiedow

My sister and I were confirmed on Palm Sunday. My cousin made our dresses. My sister had a white dress and I had a maroon one. Mine had a square neck, with a square lace yoke and trimming with little balls on it. My mother had different kinds of cloth that she had saved from dressmaking. Sometimes you'd buy something extra to make the quilts. When my aunts got together, they'd all have their quilts and show each other what they had made. —L. K.

I always brought a pretty hanky to church with a nickel tied in it. Sometimes mothers brought hankies with sugar tied up in them for the smallest children to suck on, so they would stay quiet. —A. R.

For Easter, Mother and Father would dye eggs and hide them outside, in different places. And my sister and I would have to look for them.

—L. K.

MAY • has 31 days

For, lo, the winter is past,
the rain is over and gone;
the flowers appear on the earth;
the time of the singing of birds is come,
and the voice of the turtle is heard in our land.

SONG OF SOLOMON 2:11–12

DATES AND FESTIVALS

1 *May Day.* Maypole dances and the tradition of giving baskets full of flowers come from the festival of the Roman goddess Flora.

In England, Druids celebrated this day with bonfires on the hilltops and prayers for good crops.

11 First day of the *Frost Saints' Festivals.* May 11, St. Mammertus; May 12, St. Pancras; and May 13, St. Servatus. According to legend, these saints bring cold weather when angry. German farmers call them "the three severe lords."

12 *Florence Nightingale* is born, 1820.

16 *St. Brendan's Day.* St. Brendan was an Irish monk who, according to legend, made a seven-year voyage with his crew of monks and arrived in paradise. Christopher Columbus was fascinated by the maps and stories of this voyage.

20 *Levi Strauss and Jacob Davis* patent rivet-pocket pants, 1873.

21 The American Red Cross is founded, 1881.

30 *Memorial Day.* Started by General John A. Logan in 1868.

MAY DAY

VARIABLE FEAST DAYS AND HOLIDAYS

Mother's Day, observed the second Sunday in May, was suggested in 1907 by Anna Jarvis of Philadelphia.

The counting of the Omer, a midharvest festival on the day called *Lag b'Omer* in the Jewish calendar. There are fifty days between Passover and Shabuoth. On each of the days, a sheaf, or omer, of barley is offered at the temple.

MAY ✿ the fifth month

—HARROW—

If the weather is dry, you should plow, harrow, and plant on the same day. Freshly turned soil will hold its moisture long enough to start the seed. Rows should run north to south so the sun strikes both sides.

Before Memorial Day the soil is still cold, but you may plant early peas, lettuce, and radishes. After Memorial Day sow cucumbers, squash, and melons, and set out tomato plants. It's a good idea to put aside a complete row for the birds.

SOWING SONG

One for the rook, one for the crow
One to die and one to grow.

MAY IS A GOOD TIME TO PLANT YOUR HERBS:

DILL · SAGE · SUMMER SAVORY · SWEET MARJORAM · LOVAGE · CORIANDER · FENNEL · LEMON BALM · THYME · LAVENDER · ROSEMARY · MINT · BASIL · PARSLEY · TARRAGON

Press the seeds into the soil with a board to keep the moisture in.

❧ Some Uses for Herbs ❧

• To keep ants away, plant tansy by your door.

• Chamomile tea rubbed on your skin will repel mosquitoes and soothe bee stings.

• Borage flowers are thought to cure melancholy.

• To get rid of moths, keep little bags of rosemary and wormwood in your closet.

• Pennyroyal gets rid of fleas. Other names for pennyroyal are lurk-in-the-ditch, run-by-the-ground, and, when used in meat sauces, pudding-grass.

LEATHER IS GOOD FOR PEACHES. TO ENRICH THE SOIL, BURY YOUR OLD SHOES AND BOOTS CLOSE TO YOUR TREE.

If you plan to keep bees, begin now with only one or two hives. A keg or an old barrel will do as well as an expensive hive. To keep on good terms with your bees, do not approach the hives from the front.

MAY
NAMED FOR MAIA,
*the Greek and Roman goddess
of growing and plenty*

WORTH KNOWING

🌰 Not everyone sees a man in the moon. The Japanese see a rabbit, and the Ojibwa see a boy stealing two buckets of water.

🌰 A handful of salt in the rinsing water of the wash will keep colors from running.

🌰 The giant bees of India build honeycombs reaching ten feet in height. The bee was an emblem of royalty in ancient Egypt.

🌰 Napoléon had bees painted on the walls of his bedchamber and woven into his coronation robe.

Towns with Sky Names

HALF MOON *(Montana)*
SKYLAND *(Nevada)*
LONE STAR *(Arizona)*
LOS LUNAS *(New Mexico)*
EARTH *(Texas)*
NORTH STAR ACRES *(North Dakota)*
BRIGHT STAR *(Alabama)*
OLD RED STAR *(Mississippi)*
COMET *(Virginia)*
Arkansas has both a MORNING STAR
and an EVENING STAR.
Indiana has a MOONVILLE
and a STARLIGHT.

GUARD PLANTS

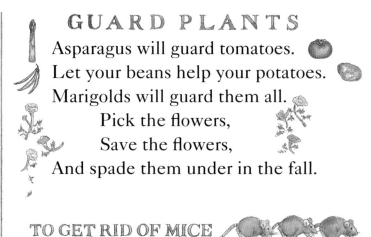

Asparagus will guard tomatoes.
Let your beans help your potatoes.
Marigolds will guard them all.
Pick the flowers,
Save the flowers,
And spade them under in the fall.

TO GET RID OF MICE

SPRINKLE WATER IN WHICH A CAT HAS BEEN WASHED OVER THE PLANTS YOU WISH TO PROTECT.

MOON PLANTING

Plant crops that grow above the ground (beans, corn, cucumbers, lettuce) in the light of the moon (the first and second quarters between new moon and full moon) when it is waxing. Plant crops that grow below the ground (beets, carrots, potatoes, turnips) in the dark of the moon (the third and fourth quarters between full moon and new moon) when it is waning.

NEW MOON | WAXING CRESCENT | FIRST QUARTER | WAXING GIBBOUS | FULL MOON | WANING GIBBOUS | FOURTH QUARTER | WANING CRESCENT

CROP ROTATION

If you want your plants to bear,
Change their planting place each year.

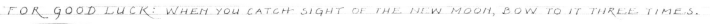
FOR GOOD LUCK: WHEN YOU CATCH SIGHT OF THE NEW MOON, BOW TO IT THREE TIMES.

THE VOICES

In the spring there were clumps of onions. I loved the onion tops on fresh bread.
—ALBERTA REIMER

THE VOICES

Sometimes I'd walk home from school—it was about a mile. My father warned me not to speak to anyone I didn't know. I'd often cut through the cemetery and then through the woods. And I'd gather shooting stars and wild geraniums and mayapples, and things like that.   —LORETTA KORFHAGE

Alton Wolf and sister Hazel with a similar idea.

We didn't have a coaster for a long time, just a tin wagon. We tried hitching a goat to it. When we got a coaster, we would work on making a racetrack on Sunday afternoons. I remember having so much fun it didn't seem fair that Sunday had to end and school was the next day.

—A. R.

Well, I was crazy to have a piano but I didn't have one, so I got a wood box and picked out pieces on that and pretended it was a piano. Finally my father bought a piano. I'd go into town to take lessons from an old woman there.   —L. K.

I had seen pictures of lily ponds in books. I saw water lilies in magazines, so I ordered one lily and one iris. I dug a hole and put in a galvanized tub. I filled it with water from the stock tank and put in the plants. The ducks kept getting into it.

I got directions for building a real lily pond, and my father made one for me. It was very unusual for him to take time to do this. On the farm he never did any work that didn't bring in income.

I ordered more lilies and bought goldfish at Woolworth. Eventually the lily pond started leaking. I kept trying to keep it filled, carrying water from the stock tank.

Finally I just took the fish to the stock tank and put them in; and they lived for five or six years. They got to be nine, ten inches long.

When we got city water, I tried filling the pond again.   —A. R.

For the icebox, you bought a chunk of ice and put it in the back.

—HAROLD WIEDOW

SUMMER

WIEDOW sisters: ALICE WOLF, VIOLET WISE,
ADENA SHEPHERD (married names)

CLARK WIEDOW

VELDA WIEDOW

ALTON WOLF *(right)* with sister, HAZEL *(middle)*, and friend

ALBERTA's father *(left)*, with wheat binder

ALBERTA's parents with family members
(mother, *far right*; father, *second from left, standing*)

ALBERTA REIMER

ALBERTA's father, wheat drill *(far right)*

ALBERTA, in carriage, with sister,
DORA, in her mother's garden

Farm where JOHN REIMER (ALBERTA's
future husband) was born

JUNE has 30 days

Yellow butterflies for corn blossoms
    (with flower-painted maidens' faces)
Blue butterflies over bean blossoms
    (with pollen-painted maidens' faces)
Yellow and blue hovering, hovering,
Wild bees singing in and out
Over all black thunder hanging
Over all downpouring rain.

HOPI KACHINA SONG FOR A CORN-PLANTING DANCE

DATES AND FESTIVALS

1 *Madame Dolphe* is the first woman to perform on a tightrope in the United States, 1819.

2 *Mrs. Nancy Johnson* patents the hand-cranked ice cream freezer, 1846.

7 *Chief Seattle* of the Suquamish and Duwamish tribes dies, 1866.

11 *King Kamehameha Day* is celebrated in Hawaii.

14 *Flag Day.* The anniversary of the day in 1777 when the Continental Congress adopted the first official American flag.

19 *The Magna Carta* is signed, 1215.

21 *Summer solstice,* the longest day of the year.

23 *Midsummer's Eve* is celebrated in Scandinavia by building bonfires on hilltops. In the far north, the sun does not set at all. According to legend, fern spores gathered on Midsummer's Eve will make you invisible if you wear them in your shoe. It is also said that a girl who gathers seven wild-flowers on Midsummer's Eve and places them on her pillow will dream of the man she will marry.

28 *Molly Pitcher* takes her wounded husband's place in the Battle of Monmouth, 1778.

VARIABLE FEAST DAYS AND HOLIDAYS

FATHER'S DAY
The third Sunday in June. Established in 1909.

SHABUOTH
The Jewish Feast of Weeks, fifty days after Passover, was originally called the Feast of the Harvest. It has come to honor the day the Jews received the Ten Commandments.

Flower Rose

FARMER'S CALENDAR

HARVEST SCHEDULE

	May	June	July	Aug.	Sept.	Oct.	Nov.
Apples				▨	▨		
Blueberries			▨	▨			
Melons				▨	▨		
Cherries		▨					
Grapes				▨	▨		
Peaches			▨	▨	▨		
Pears				▨	▨		
Plums				▨	▨		
Raspberries			▨	▨			
Strawberries		▨					
Asparagus	▨						
Beans		▨	▨	▨	▨		
Beets		▨	▨	▨	▨	▨	
Broccoli & Cabbage		▨			▨	▨	
Carrots			▨	▨	▨	▨	
Cauliflower			▨	▨	▨	▨	
Celery			▨	▨	▨	▨	
Corn			▨	▨	▨		
Cucumbers			▨	▨	▨		
Lettuce		▨	▨	▨	▨		
Onions			▨	▨	▨	▨	
Peas		▨	▨				
Peppers & Eggplant				▨	▨		
Potatoes			▨	▨	▨	▨	
Pumpkins					▨	▨	
Radishes	▨	▨	▨	▨	▨		
Rhubarb	▨	▨	▨				
Spinach	▨	▨		▨	▨		
Squash			▨	▨	▨	▨	
Tomatoes			▨	▨	▨		

Plant late crops: squash, fall cabbages, rutabagas, and corn. Plant pumpkins at the edge of your cornfields to discourage raccoons; they dislike getting tangled in the vines.

Start your kitchen garden. Remember to make successive plantings of sweet corn, beans, peas, tomatoes, lettuce, and beets.

HOW TO KEEP MOLES OUT OF YOUR GARDEN:

Sink empty bottles into the ground around the molehills, leaving a couple of inches of the necks showing above the soil. The wind blowing over the bottles will make a hollow sound, to the great annoyance of the moles.

Beans do well when planted in a mixture of soil and hair.

Pumpkins, cucumbers, and pole beans do not like to be planted near potatoes.

Spray your cucumber vines with sugar water. This will attract bees, and the vines will set more cucumbers.

IN 1902 A FRENCH NATURALIST CLAIMED THAT IF ALL THE BIRDS SHOULD DISAPPEAR, HUMANS COULD NOT SURVIVE BEYOND NINE YEARS. SLUGS AND INSECTS WOULD DEVOUR ORCHARDS AND CROPS.

GOOD BUGS FOR GARDENERS
these bugs destroy other bugs:

Doodlebug, ladybug, predaceous mite,
   guard my garden day and night.
Praying mantis, syrphid fly,
   keep a predatory eye
On what tries to gnaw and burrow
   through the seedlings in this furrow.

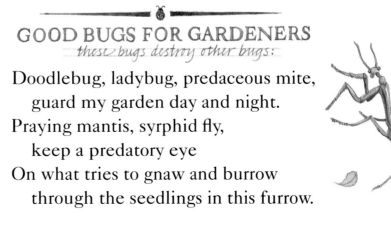

WORTH KNOWING

- The Oneota were Wisconsin's first farmers. They planted their corn on raised ridges. The ditches between the ridges allowed the fields to drain.

- Gardeners in ancient Greece wrote messages to the mice, requesting them to leave their gardens.

- Many glacial lakes in Wisconsin are connected by underground rivers. The Chippewa say that what is lost in one lake will sometimes turn up in another.

Flowers

SOME EDIBLE FLOWERS TO PLANT:
Nasturtiums, squash blossoms, daylilies, violets, and chrysanthemums. Pick them early in the day and keep them in cold water till you are ready to eat them.

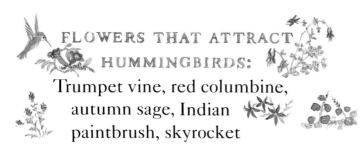

FLOWERS THAT ATTRACT HUMMINGBIRDS:
Trumpet vine, red columbine, autumn sage, Indian paintbrush, skyrocket

Put old tea leaves on the soil around your roses to increase their fragrance. Plant parsley near roses for the same reason.

WEATHER WISE

RAINBOW WEATHER:
If green is the strongest color, rain will continue. If red, there will be wind and rain. If blue, the air will be clear.

There is a game called *Los Colores* about the rainbow and St. Inez:

Draw a large circle on the ground for home base. Choose one player to be *la vieja Ines* (St. Inez), and another to be *la madre* (the Mother, or Rainbow). The other players are *los colores*, the colors. *La madre* gives them their names: Red, Yellow, Blue, and so on.

La madre and *los colores* stand opposite St. Inez, who comes up and pretends to knock at the door. *Tan, tan.* (Knock, knock.) She asks for a color and the one whose color is named runs away. If he reaches home base before St. Inez catches him, *la madre* gives him a new color name and he stays in the game. When all the colors have been caught, St. Inez chases *la madre*. When *la madre* is caught, the game is over.

THE VOICES

h, there was a lot of visiting. The men would play cards. My father's birthday was celebrated in summertime. There was a big table set up outside and chairs around that. The Milwaukee people were always very special, so they'd be seated first, and they gorged themselves on chicken. And maybe the wings would be left for us children to eat. Most of the women were busy serving the men.

—LORETTA KORFHAGE

T H E   V O I C E S

My mother dyed her wedding dress indigo after the wedding so she could wear it for every day.
—ALBERTA REIMER

Usually my mother churned the butter, but sometimes I would ask to help churn, and I'd say, "Isn't this long enough? Isn't this long enough?" The same with the washing. First Mother heated water on the stove and boiled the clothes. Then she put them in the washing machine. It wasn't electric. There was a lever that I had to push back and forth. And I'd say, "Oh, aren't they washed enough now? Haven't they been washed long enough?"
—L. K.

When I think about it, we never had running water or a bathroom. In the summertime we'd go out in that old house over there and take our bath. We had one of those big oval tubs and a water heater that we used. We had to carry the water over and fill up the tub.
—ALTON WOLF

Behind the house, toward the main road, was my mother's garden. She had vegetables, but she was known for her flowers. She had peonies that were from roots my grandparents brought from Russia. They were a purplish red, very unusual.

There was a double row of tiger lilies. We would pull out the centers and paint our faces with the black pollen. And there were red-and-white peppermint tulips, pink double roses, and yellow roses, which my mother always told us not to bother picking because they wouldn't last in the house.

We had red poppies, and nasturtiums, which my mother called *blick durch den Zaun*, which meant "look through the fence." She called the impatiens *Alltag*—I guess because they bloomed all day.

We didn't have running water, so we carried buckets filled with water from the stock tanks to water the flowers.
—A. R.

To reach the best fishing spot, you had to cross a bridge. Sometimes the local boys swam there in the nude. We always made quite a lot of noise before we got to the bridge, to give them time to get out of the way.
—L. K.

JULY has 31 days

The wind begun to rock the Grass
With threatening Tunes and low—
He threw a Menace at the Earth—
A Menace at the Sky.

The Leaves unhooked themselves
    from Trees—
And started all abroad
The Dust did scoop itself like Hands
And threw away the Road.

The Wagons quickened on the Streets,
The Thunder hurried slow—
The Lightning showed a Yellow Beak
And then a livid Claw.

The Birds put up the Bars to Nests—
The Cattle fled to Barns—
There came one drop of Giant Rain
And then as if the Hands

That held the Dams had parted hold
The Waters Wrecked the Sky,
But overlooked my Father's House—
Just quartering a Tree—

Emily Dickinson

DATES AND FESTIVALS

1   *Canada Day*

3   *Dog days.* Forty days of hot weather named for Sirius, the Dog Star. It was believed that dogs went mad during this time.

4   *Independence Day,* 1776. Thomas Jefferson buys his first thermometer. His weather report states that July 4, 1776, was cloudy, with a temperature of seventy-six degrees at 2 P.M.

5   *P. T. Barnum* is born, 1910.

6   *Frida Kahlo,* Mexican painter, is born, 1907.

8   The Liberty Bell cracks, 1835.

9   The corncob pipe is patented, 1878.

11   *John Quincy Adams* is born, 1767.
Author *Susan Warner* is born, 1819. Her book *The Wide, Wide World* was the first novel to sell one million copies in the United States.

15   *St. Swithin's Day.* St. Swithin, a ninth-century English bishop, wanted to be buried in the churchyard after his death. According to legend, an attempt on this day in the year 971 to move his bones from the churchyard to the cathedral was thwarted by forty days of rain.

*If rain falls on St. Swithin's Day
For forty days the rain will stay.*

22   Poet *Emma Lazarus,* whose words are inscribed at the base of the Statue of Liberty, is born, 1849.

23   *Henry David Thoreau* refuses to pay the poll tax and is arrested, 1846.

24   Mormons, led by *Brigham Young,* reach Salt Lake, 1847.
Amelia Earhart is born, 1898.

JULY

the seventh month

flower ~ water lily

BIRTHSTONE
• ruby FOR CONTENTMENT

FARMER'S CALENDAR

This is the month for harvesting much of your grass and wheat, and for mowing your hayfields, turning the hay to dry it, raking it, and building the load on the hay wagon for the horse to draw it into the barn.

To keep your hens laying, give them free range for at least part of the day.

Watch out for rattlesnakes. More people are bitten in July than in any other month.

At the end of the day, nothing refreshes like a bath. Every farmhouse should have one good-sized bathtub and plenty of water.

The deer are growing their new antlers this month.

Make a second planting of vegetables—a fall crop.

In the woodlands and ravines, look for the pale blue blossoms of the BELLFLOWERS.

Remember the old saying: "Anything that grows in the summer will rot in the winter." When you make your compost heap, alternate layers of vegetation—potato tops, swamp grass, ferns, sod—with manure from the stable and the hog pen.

BE SURE YOUR DUCKS HAVE WATER, BOTH MORNING AND NIGHT.

WORTH KNOWING

A legend about St. Isidore:

St. Isidore was a very good farmer and a pious man. One Sunday his wife made him work, but as he was planting his fields, the Lord spoke to him, telling him that he should not work on Sunday.

"I'm sorry," said Isidore, "but I have to work."

The Lord told Isidore He would send a hailstorm.

"I'm not afraid of hail," said Isidore, and he kept on working.

The Lord told Isidore He would send a plague of locusts.

"I'm not afraid of locusts," said Isidore, and he kept on working.

Then the Lord told Isidore to stop working, or He would send him a bad neighbor. This Isidore couldn't stand, so he left his work and went to Mass. When he returned, he discovered that an angel had finished planting his fields.

JULY

NAMED FOR JULIUS CAESAR
the Roman Emperor

WORTH KNOWING

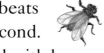

TOMATOES WERE ONCE CONSIDERED POISONOUS

- It is temperature, more than light, that ripens tomatoes.
- The largest tomato on record weighed 7 pounds, 12 ounces.
- One lightning bolt can carry a million volts.
- The common housefly beats its wings 190 times a second.
- Cowslip conserve mixed with hog grease was once a remedy for sunburn.

WORTH COOKING

Raspberry Shrub

3 pints raspberries
1 1/2 cups sugar
2 cups water
1 cup lemon juice
2 quarts ice water
crushed ice

Combine raspberries, sugar, and the 2 cups water in a large saucepan and cook over medium heat for 10 minutes, stirring frequently. Pour through a strainer and let cool. Add lemon juice and ice water. Pour over crushed ice in tall, frosted glasses.

WEATHER WISE

- It's said that the rattlesnake never lets its rattles get wet. If you are a fiddler, keep rattles in your fiddle case to protect its strings from the damp.
- When rattlesnakes head for higher ground, look out for rain.
- When frogs croak loud and long, they are "calling for water," and you can expect rain.
- When cream and milk turn sour at night, listen for thunder.
- To determine how far you are from a storm's center, count the seconds between the time you see lightning and the time you hear thunder. Five seconds equals one mile.
- "Even the lightning did us no harm, for whenever it came too close, mothers and grandmothers in every tipi put cedar leaves on the coals and their magic kept danger away." —*Chief Luther Standing Bear* TETON SIOUX
- "Earth sweats" are beads of moisture that appear on china, brick, stone, wood, and metal objects when the humidity is rising. Look for rain.

BEE BALM, WHICH BLOOMS THIS MONTH, IS ALSO CALLED OSWEGO TEA, AFTER THE NATIVE AMERICANS WHO DRANK TEA MADE FROM IT.

THE VOICES

I remember Grossmutter told me about the time a terrible windstorm came up and Uncle Henry was outside, and she couldn't get the door open to let him back in the house on account of the wind. So Uncle Henry lay on the ground and hung on to the grass, and the storm just whipped him up and down like a rug and passed over him. —HAROLD WIEDOW

THE VOICES

Tornadoes came in the spring. Just before one came it would be very still, which was not very common. There would be no breeze, and the air seemed very heavy.

We'd look toward the east, and the sky would be very dark. There was a sound of rumbling like a big train or truck.

We all had to go in the house. My father would stand at the front porch, and he kept his eye on the horse barn. If that went, he knew to send us to the cellar, to a spot where nothing heavy, like the stove, was above us. I remember my father standing at the screen door looking out. I always watched the expression on his face.　　—ALBERTA REIMER

The hailstorm hit where Alice and her folks lived. Where they lived the corn was just as beautiful as could be, and fifteen minutes later you couldn't hardly see the stubs in the field. That's how bad it was. It seemed like whenever a storm went through, we'd get some of it.　　—ALTON WOLF

One time a tornado hit your dad's farm. It lifted the barn and shifted it on its foundation. It came through a window of the house, scattered pots and pans, and went out.

Another farm, which we rented to a family, had a storm cellar outside. The family was in it during a storm and realized the water was coming in so fast it was up to the neck of their five-year-old boy. Their house and barn were flattened. Clothes and mattresses were lying in the trees.

I remember a baby was lifted up and found dead in a ditch.　　—A. R.

There was only one thing we were afraid of. When there was an electrical storm, we'd watch the buildings carefully. If there was a hard crack of thunder, we'd watch to see if it brought fire down along the road.　　—LORETTA KORFHAGE

At night if there were storms my mother would wake us and light kerosene lamps. Usually it was just thunder and lightning.　　—A. R.

The day was bright when I went into the planted field
Alone I wandered in the planted field

It was the time of the second hoeing

A maiden appeared and clasped me about the neck saying
    When you leave this earth for the new world above
    we want to follow you

I looked for the maiden
but saw only the long leaves of corn
twined round my shoulders

I understood it was the spirit of the corn
speaking
she the sustainer of life.

"A VISION OF HANDSOME LAKE," SENECA

DATES AND FESTIVALS

1 *Lammas Day.* Summer is half gone. In medieval England a loaf of bread made from the first cutting of wheat was brought to church and blessed.

Francis Scott Key, who wrote "The Star Spangled Banner," is born, 1779.

Harriet Quimby passes the Aero Club test, becoming the first licensed woman pilot in the United States, 1911.

3 *Columbus* sails from Spain, 1492.

4 *Susanna Wright,* pioneer from Pennsylvania, scribe and physician to the Conestoga, is born, 1697.

13 *Annie Oakley* is born, 1860.

18 *Virginia Dare,* the first child of English parents born in America, 1587.

19 *Gail Borden* patents the process for condensing milk, 1856.

22 The *Red Cross* is founded, 1864.

24 Day of *St. Bartholomew,* patron saint of butchers, tanners, and beekeepers. This day ends the forty days of rain forecast by a wet St. Swithin's Day and brings the "cold dew," the cool autumn weather.

*All the tears St. Swithin can cry
St. Bartholomew's mantle can wipe dry.*

Mt. Vesuvius erupts and destroys the cities of Pompeii and Herculaneum, A.D. 79.

28 *Pedro Menéndez de Avilés* enters the harbor he names for St. Augustine, 1565.

Elizabeth Ann "Mother" Seton, the first American Roman Catholic saint, is born in New York, 1774.

AUGUST • the eighth month

flower
poppy

BIRTHSTONE
peridot
FOR
MARRIED HAPPINESS

FARMER'S CALENDAR

Check your fences to keep your cows from nibbling the fodder corn in your neighbor's field.

After the middle of the month, you can prepare your grassland for seeding. Sow turnips at the beginning of the month for a winter crop.

Early potatoes, squash, and onions are coming in. When digging your potatoes, dry them in the sun only long enough for them to get dusty. Potatoes will not keep well if left too long in the sun.

When picking your early apples, handle them as carefully as peaches, as they are not as hard as the "keeping" varieties.

When you are out walking, look for arrowleaf along sluggish streams. Native Americans called the potato-like tubers on its roots *wapato*.

If you have a stream of good water on your land, build an ice house so when the water freezes you can harvest the ice.

"We always give the Great Spirit something. I think that is good. We see the sun, we give him something, and the moon and the earth, we give them something."
—*Blackfoot*, CROW CHIEF, 1873

WEATHER WISE

When grass is dry in morning light,
Look for rain before the night;
When the dew is on the grass,
Rain will never come to pass.

If spiders spin during the rain, the storm will pass quickly.

If a cat lies with its back to the stove or scratches on the wall, there's a good chance of rain.

If coyotes howl on the hills after sunrise, it will rain.

If two burros braying after dusk are answered by one or more burros braying some distance away, it will rain before morning.

On Saturday night I lost my wife,
And where do you think I found her?
Up in the moon, singing a tune,
And all the stars around her.

AUGUST •

NAMED FOR AUGUSTUS CAESAR
the Roman Emperor

WORTH KNOWING

- A cloth soaked in white vinegar or chilled tea will ease the pain of sunburn.
- An ointment made from elderberry flowers will heal the sores on your animals.
- Some odd cures for a toothache:
    Pick your teeth with the nail of the middle toe of an owl.
    Put on your left shoe first.
- Sunflowers were tended and harvested in North America before 23,000 B.C.
- August offers you a chance to observe meteors.
- The Scandinavian miners who came to the Lake Superior region missed the pets they'd left behind. One man brought over a few cats to sell and ended up making his fortune with all the kittens that were born during the voyage.

WORTH COOKING

Corn Pudding

3 heaping cups fresh corn kernels
   (about 4 medium ears)
3 eggs, well beaten
3 tbsp. unbleached white flour
1 tsp. salt, or to taste
2 tbsp. butter, melted
1 cup whole milk

   Preheat the oven to 325°.
   Plunge the corn into boiling water. Take care not to overcook. When it's cool enough to handle, scrape the kernels off with a sharp knife and place them in a mixing bowl. Add the salt, milk, eggs, flour, and melted butter, and mix together thoroughly.
   Pour the mixture into an oiled 1 1/2-quart casserole. Bake for 1 hour, or until the top is golden brown and the pudding is set.

BARN CATS

*Barn cats are wild. They run away
And hide themselves behind the hay.
They will not let you stroke their fur.
They'd rather fight than sit and purr.
They don't drink milk like other cats.*

*They live on mice and owls and rats.
I'm glad that all cats aren't the same,
I like them best when they are tame.
A house cat makes a better pet
Than any barn cat you can get.*

ELIZABETH WHERRY

THE VOICES

When my dad started farming, you bought machinery and you expected it to last a lifetime.
—HAROLD WIEDOW

THE VOICES

My father had a fanning mill that took the chaff and bugs out of the grain, and he'd let me run that. He also had a machine to sharpen instruments. There'd be water in the trough for this grindstone, and I'd have to turn the wheel on the grindstone to sharpen the knives.

There was a crew that went around from one farm to the next to thrash. My father would say, "Well, we'll be having the thrashers on such and such a day."

The thrashing crew would bring the machine to a place between the house and the barn. Of course, that was a busy time because we had quite a few to feed, about thirty or thirty-five. We had a nice tree out in the back, and my father and mother arranged to have a pail of water there so the men could wash their hands. Some of the men were in a hurry to get a place at the table.

I remember I used to sit on the back steps and peel potatoes. And I'd throw bits of potato peel out because the chickens loved that. And they'd come running. They'd come and sing for me to give them some potato peels.

—LORETTA KORFHAGE

One day as I played under the cedar trees, I planted a seedling. And I played farm there. I made my own house. It had a tin roof. I borrowed my brother's tin farm animals and tractor. I had a tin box that was used for baby chicks as my barn. I brought buckets of water from the stock tank to make rivers, but they always dried up. When my mother took a nap in the afternoons, I would go play there. It was cool in the shade.

—ALBERTA REIMER

I'd mow the lawn. I had to mow a path from the house to the barn and the chicken house, and I thought it looked so nice I mowed a strip to the chicken house and another one to the pig pen, and then I mowed a strip to the part of the barn where we kept the cows. That's just the way it went. I kept making the path wider and wider. I'd mow one strip and another strip, and pretty soon the whole backyard was mowed.

—L. K.

My father had different fields of grain, and he'd cut the grain and bind it up in bundles until the thrashers could come and thrash it. My mother would help shock the grain and the corn, and stack bales of hay, and drive the horses into the barn. We had two big workhorses to draw the binder or other heavy machinery, and a smaller white horse named Polly we hitched alongside to help out when we needed more horses.

—L. K.

FALL

Above: X marks the spot for the WIEDOW homeplace.

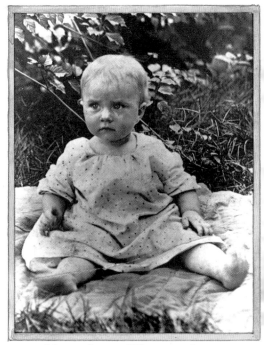

Above: ALICE WIEDOW, future MRS. ALTON WOLF

LORETTA KORFHAGE

MRS. BEN FROESE *(right)*, ALBERTA REIMER's aunt, cleaning hog intestines

ALBERTA REIMER *(right)* with brother, HARRY

Above: ALTON WOLF *(far left)*

Left: ALTON WOLF

ALBERTA REIMER *(second row, far left)* with first and second grades

ALBERTA's school

JOHNNY REIMER, ALBERTA's future husband *(front row, fourth from right)*

VELDA WIEDOW *(left)* and family

SEPTEMBER 🍎 has 30 days

Follow the drinking gourd!
Follow the drinking gourd.
For the old man is a-waiting for to carry you to freedom
If you follow the drinking gourd.

When the sun comes back, and the first quail calls,
Follow the drinking gourd.
For the old man is a-waiting for to carry you to freedom
If you follow the drinking gourd.

AFRICAN AMERICAN FOLK SONG

DATES AND FESTIVALS

1 *Velda Wiedow* is born, 1890.

2 Hawaiian *Queen Liliuokalani* is born, 1838. HER SONG, "ALOHA OE" BECAME THE TRADITIONAL FAREWELL SONG.

4 *George Eastman* patents the Kodak camera, 1888.

6 Oberlin becomes the first college to admit women on an equal footing with men, 1837. OBERLIN

8 Between 6,000 and 7,200 people are killed in a hurricane when a 20-foot tidal wave engulfs Galveston, Texas, 1900.

12 *Loretta Korfhage* is born, 1898.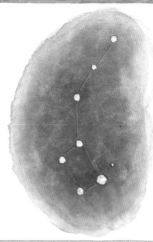

14 Gregorian calendar adopted, 1752.
Nutting Day in England. According to legend, the devil would hold down the branches on this day while you harvested the nuts. To say "The sky is as black as the devil's nutting bag" is to predict a storm.

15 *Clark Wiedow* is born, 1915.
The day on which ladybugs are honored for their good service to gardeners during the growing season.

16 Shawmut, Massachusetts, is renamed Boston, 1630.

22 *Elsie Allen,* Pomo basket maker, is born, 1899.
The ice cream cone is patented, 1903.

23 *Victoria Woodhull,* first woman candidate for the U.S. presidency, is born, 1838. ★EQUAL RIGHTS PARTY★
The fall equinox. One of the two times in the year when day and night are equal.

29 **Day of** *St. Michael the Archangel*
A tree planted at Michaelmas Will surely not go amiss.

VARIABLE FEAST DAYS AND HOLIDAYS

THE HIGH HOLIDAYS

The first ten days of the Jewish year open with Rosh Hashanah and the blowing of the shofar, or ram's horn. Rosh Hashanah, also called Day of Remembrance, is a day of prayer and repentance. A traditional food is apples dipped in honey. The High Holidays end with Yom Kippur, the Day of Atonement, a day of fasting and reconciliation.

SEPTEMBER 🍎 the ninth month

LABOR DAY

Observed the first Monday in September, Labor Day was proposed in 1882 by Peter McGuire, president of the United Brotherhood of Carpenters and Joiners.

flower
morning glory

FARMER'S CALENDAR

BIRTHSTONE
• *sapphire*
FOR
CLEAR THINKING

September is a busy month. There are beans and peas to harvest and grain to thrash. Your beets and carrots and turnips are growing fast—and so are the weeds.

Get rid of the large rocks that might stand in the way of the plow when you are sowing your winter wheat. If the weather is moist, you can do the plowing early and use the harrow to kill seedling weeds.

Save the best ears of sweet corn from your best hills for seed next year.

Pick up your windfall apples. Those not fit for making cider can be fed to the pigs. When the tops of your potato plants die, your potatoes are ready to dig and put in a cool cellar for keeping.

WORTH KNOWING

 Exposing your potatoes to the light turns the skins green. Green potatoes are poisonous. Boil them and use the water as an insect killer in the garden.

 Popcorn pops because the moisture in the kernel turns to steam when it is heated and bursts the outer skin.

Fall apples (September to November):

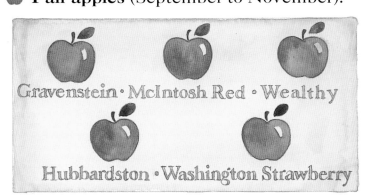

Gravenstein • McIntosh Red • Wealthy

Hubbardston • Washington Strawberry

When you can fruits and vegetables, heat the jars to 165° for fifteen minutes. Let the jars stand one or two days and heat them twice more to be sure of killing all germs. Keep doors and windows closed against drafts that might break the jars.

STORING APPLES:

Do not pick fruit that's still wet. Pick apples in the afternoon and lay them in a cool, dry space for two weeks. Wrap each one in tissue or newspaper and set on shelves or open trays, with none of them touching, in the cellar or shed.

To eat an apple going to bed
Will make the doctor beg his bread.

SEPTEMBER

NAMED FOR THE LATIN WORD FOR SEVEN
It was the seventh month of the Roman calendar before July and August were added.

WORTH KNOWING

- The squirrel population of Olney, Illinois, includes more than a thousand albinos.
- Millions of passenger pigeons once filled the skies of North America. When they flew north in the spring, an estimated three or four billion of them darkened the sky. One flock flying south was reported to be a mile wide and 240 miles long. By 1900 they were extinct. The last known passenger pigeon was killed in Ohio by a boy with a BB gun.
- Slaves escaping on the Underground Railroad used songs as a code for instructions and information. The hymn "Follow the Risen Lord" was sung as "Follow the Drinking Gourd." The "gourd" is the Little Dipper, which includes the North Star.
- One of the greatest "conductors" of the Underground Railroad was Harriet Tubman, who brought more than three hundred slaves to freedom.
- In England the last sheaf cut from the harvest was called the corn dolly. It was decorated with flowers and ribbons and carried home on the last wagonload. The next year it was burned and its ashes were plowed into the soil.

WORTH COOKING

 ### *Apple Pandowdy*

Fill a pot with sliced apples.
Add 1 cup molasses, 1 cup sugar, 1 cup water, 1 tsp. cloves, 1 tsp. cinnamon.
Cover with baking-powder biscuit crust, sloping it over the sides of the pot.
Bake slowly overnight. In the morning break the crust into the apples and eat with cream.

Blueberry Strum

Crush 1 quart berries with 1 cup sugar.
Stir in cubed white bread from 12 slices of a day-old loaf.
Chill and serve in deep bowls with milk or cream.
Add freshly grated nutmeg to taste.

FOOD FOR THOUGHT

"Unfortunately too many farm women are putting their spare time on tatting, crocheting, embroidery, and the like.... You must bar them all at a stroke, for they keep you indoors and use up your precious eyesight." —*Nellie Kedzie Jones*

THE VOICES

We didn't have to walk any further than two miles to school. We didn't have buses at that time. Most of my school days I drove a horse to school. We had a barn in town we rented, and we'd put the horse there throughout the day. After school you'd pick the horse up and come home.

—ALTON WOLF

THE VOICES

I started school when I was seven and spoke very little English. My sister, who was four years older, taught me English. The school was a square brick building. The floors were oiled. There were eight grades, but two grades were together. The high school was upstairs.

—ALBERTA REIMER

In first grade we did a lot of mat work. We had colored paper cut in strips, and we wove it into mats. We'd make whatever we could out of those strips, and then we'd have to take them apart again.

—LORETTA KORFHAGE

My first teacher was Miss Miller. She was a pretty blond. On the first day she wore a pink top and a white pleated skirt. She wasn't Mennonite like us. I drew a horse on the chalkboard. She liked it and left it there. Charles Wilson erased it.   —A. R.

After sixth grade I went to parochial school, St. Paul's Lutheran. My father and mother wanted me to learn catechism for confirmation. I was scared to death of the teacher because I'd seen him lay the boys across the piano stool and hit them. He'd spank them with a ruler or a strap. He had all gold teeth, and I just hated to see him smile. My father told him that I was very nervous and he shouldn't spank me.

—L. K.

I thought surely my father and mother would give me a party or do something special for my sixteenth birthday. But when I came home from school, there was no party. My father said, "Today you pick up the chips around the woodpile." The first time I had a birthday party was after Roy and I were married. Roy gave me a surprise party.

—L. K.

I had an old husking peg that Dad fixed smaller to fit my hand when I used to help husk corn the first year we were married— and other years, later, when the kids helped husk, too, or the smaller ones rode in the wagon. I would get up early and put a chicken in the oil-stove oven and have the potatoes peeled and bread all baked, ready in the big stone jar in the pantry. Butter churned, and canned fruit in the basement I could open quick so we could hurry back to the fields, then wash all those dishes at night.

—VELDA WIEDOW

OCTOBER  has 31 days

> If fresh meat be wanting to fill up our dish
> We have carrots and pumpkins and turnips and fish;
> We have pumpkins at morning and pumpkins at noon;
> If it was not for pumpkins, we should be undone.
>
> *Anonymous*

DATES AND FESTIVALS

1 Astronomer *Maria Mitchell* discovers a comet, 1847.

2 *Guardian Angels Day*

3 *Black Hawk,* warrior and Sauk chief who tried to confederate Indian tribes in a war against the Americans, dies, 1838.

4 *St. Francis of Assisi's Day*

5 *Chief Joseph* and 414 Nez Percé Indians surrender at Bear Paw Mountain, 1877: "Hear me, my chiefs, I am tired; my heart is sick and sad. From where the sun now stands, I will fight no more forever."

12 *Columbus Day.* Columbus reaches the Bahamas, 1492.

14 *William Penn,* Quaker leader and founder of the colony of Pennsylvania, is born, 1644.

15 *Day of St. Gerard,* patron saint of mothers. It is said that his blessing on a poor family's small wheat harvest caused it to last miraculously for a year.

16 Comanche chief *Ten Bears* gives a speech about reservation life, 1867: "I was born upon the prairie where the wind blew free and there was nothing to break the light of the sun. . . . I want to die there and not within walls."

18 ***Day of*** *St. Luke,* a doctor, writer, and painter. St. Luke is the patron saint of artists. If the four days around his day are warm and clear, they are called St. Luke's Little Summer.

31 Hallowe'en. All Hallow's Eve, Night of the Dead, last day of the Celtic year. On this night, the Fairy Court rides at midnight. It is also the eve of the Druid feast of Samhain, Lord of Death, when the dead are thought to appear at midnight.

VARIABLE FEAST DAYS AND HOLIDAYS

SUKKOT

The Festival of Tabernacles. Jews remember the Israelites' forty years of wandering in the wilderness after their escape from slavery in Egypt. The festival was observed by the building of a temporary home, a small tabernacle of wood or cloth, open to the sky and covered only with branches.

OCTOBER · the tenth month

flower
hop

FARMER'S CALENDAR

BIRTHSTONE
opal
FOR HOPE

A good farm should be as neat as a lady's parlor.

Before the ground freezes, plow all the land you plan to cultivate next spring. If ground is left rough, frost can more easily break the soil into a fine powder.

Your hens will be laying freely now. Separate the best layers from the others, since the food requirements will be different.

Let your hogs harvest the chestnuts, acorns, and beechnuts on the forest floor.

There will soon be a demand for good turkeys. If you plan to raise turkeys for the coming year, give special care to the young birds when they are molting. Do not let them run free in wet weather or till the dew has dried on the grass.

Pick your winter apples before they become too ripe. The good fruit should be handled carefully. A bruised apple will not keep well and injures those next to it. Keep apples in a cool cellar, but do not allow them to freeze. Your fruit cellar may be a cave or a room dug into a hill.

The turnips and parsnips you pick in the fall can be packed in barrels of sand and kept in your root cellar or some other cool, dark place.

Give your bees special care. They have finished their year's work. Take off the super (the removable upper section of the hive) and examine the swarms. If the hive without the super does not weigh at least forty pounds, feed your bees a syrup made from granulated sugar to bring them up to this weight, and prepare them for winter.

Take time to put the farm in order. Prune bushes away from your fences, repair holes in the barn, and put all tools back in their proper places.

WORTH KNOWING

- Barrow, Alaska, averages eight frost-free days per year.
- How to grow a really big pumpkin: Pick all the blossoms and fruits but one. All the plant's strength will go into that one fruit.
- The largest pumpkin on record weighed 827 pounds. It was grown by Norm L. Craven of Stouffville, Ontario.
- In 1848 John Curtis and his brother manufactured the first chewing gum, State of Maine Pure Spruce Gum, in Bangor, Maine.

OCTOBER

NAMED FOR THE LATIN WORD FOR EIGHT
*It was the eighth month in the Roman year
before July and August were introduced.*

WORTH KNOWING

- In China and Japan peachwood is thought to protect children from evil spirits.
- Loggers in the North Woods tell tales about the hodag, which is said to be seven feet long and thirty inches tall, with twelve horns down its spine, horns on its head, razor-sharp claws, green-glowing eyes, and a ten-inch spike at the end of its tail. It preys on white bulldogs.

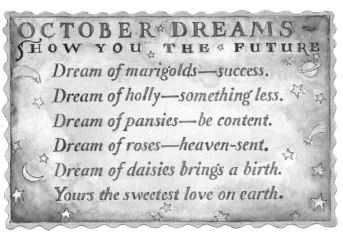

OCTOBER DREAMS ~
SHOW YOU THE FUTURE

Dream of marigolds—success.
Dream of holly—something less.
Dream of pansies—be content.
Dream of roses—heaven-sent.
Dream of daisies brings a birth.
Yours the sweetest love on earth.

WEATHER WISE

- If prairie dogs pile dirt around the entrances of their burrows, expect a downpour.

WORTH COOKING

Pumpkin Fudge

2 cups sugar
1/4 tsp. pumpkin pie spice
2 tbsp. canned pumpkin
1/2 cup condensed milk
1/4 tsp. cornstarch
1/2 tsp. vanilla
a pinch of salt

In a heavy-bottomed saucepan combine all ingredients except vanilla. Cook over medium heat, stirring constantly until mixture forms a soft ball. (Drop from a spoon into a glass of tap water.) Then add vanilla and let mixture cool to lukewarm. Heat mixture until creamy. Pour into a buttered 8" x 8" pan and cut into squares.

COW FACTS

- Until a female calf gives birth for the first time, she is called a heifer. After that first birth, her birthdays are recorded and she is called a cow.

THE VOICES

We had a black dog named Bruno. He was a wonderful watchdog. He usually slept in the woodshed, which had a big hook on the door so it couldn't be opened from the outside. One night somebody tried to open it, and Bruno yipped right away. By the time my father was dressed and outside, there was no sign of anybody. Bruno sniffed them as far as the woods. My father didn't want Bruno in the woods because there might be hunters or wolves that would fight him. He called Bruno back so he wouldn't get harmed.

—LORETTA KORFHAGE

THE VOICES

There was a prairie dog village in one of the fields near the farm. My father wanted to get rid of the prairie dogs because the horses would step in the holes and get hurt. The village was near two round ponds. These were buffalo wallows, formed by buffalos rolling to get the dirt off. Soft grass grew there, which the cows would not eat, and after the rain they would fill up with water.

My father put poison in the ponds to try and kill the prairie dogs. One day my brother, Harry, and his close friend Raymond, who lived across the street, saw the horses near the ponds. They ran out to try and scare away the horses, but Harry got kicked. All the skin from one side of his face got pushed back. Raymond got so scared he crawled under the fence and ran home. Harry walked all the way home. By the time he got there, his overalls were all covered with blood. My mother looked out the window and saw him. My father was in town, so she called the store and told them to locate him. There was a doctor in Buhler, luckily, who came.

I spent hours with Harry every day. He was all bandaged up. I would read to him and try to say funny things. I just wanted to make him happy. —ALBERTA REIMER

We had two butternut trees in the yard, and they were quite tall. When the nuts fell down, we picked them up and put newspapers on the floor and put the nuts on them to dry out. When they got good and dry, we'd take the outer shell off. They were still hard to crack, but we'd ask my father to crack them open. They tasted delicious to us.

—L. K.

I had a playhouse out in back made of planks, with English ivy growing on it. There was an apple tree out there.

The south road had Osage orange trees. I'd gather them and make dolls. I used sticks for their feet and made clothes for them. —A. R.

I often say I'm probably the oldest reader of *Good Housekeeping*, because I was ten years old when my father and mother had me read it to them. I don't know if they just liked to hear me read or if they wanted to give me practice in reading.

—L. K.

NOVEMBER · has 30 days

Look at the stars! look, look up at the skies!
O look at all the fire-folk sitting in the air!
The bright boroughs, the circle-citadels there!
Down in the dim woods the diamond delves! the elves'-eyes!
The grey lawns cold where gold, where quickgold lies!

Gerard Manley Hopkins,
THE STARLIGHT NIGHT

DATES AND FESTIVALS

1 *All Saints' Day.* A day of prayer for the saints in paradise. In Mexico it's called the Day of the Dead. On the first and second of November, the dead are said to have divine permission to visit friends and relatives on earth.

2 *All Souls' Day.* A day of prayer for the souls in purgatory. Mexican families go to the graveyard with offerings of food, flowers, and incense. Sometimes brass bands serenade the dead.

9 *Benjamin Banneker,* almanac publisher, is born, 1731. He made the first clock built in the United States.

19 Lincoln's address at Gettysburg, 1863.

20 *St. Edmund's Day.* St. Edmund is the patron saint of farmers and gardeners.

21 The Pilgrims sign the Mayflower Compact, in which everyone agrees to establish the colony at Plymouth.

22 *Day of St. Cecilia,* patron saint of music. She is said to have played the harp so beautifully that an angel flew down to hear her.

25 The Kiowa defeat Kit Carson and his New Mexico Volunteers at Adobe Walls in the Texas Panhandle, 1864.

26 *Sojourner Truth,* abolitionist and preacher, dies, 1883.

29 *Louisa May Alcott* is born, 1832.

30 *Mark Twain* is born, 1835.
St. Andrew's Day. St. Andrew is the patron saint of Scotland.

VARIABLE FEAST DAYS AND HOLIDAYS

THANKSGIVING

ADVENT

Advent marks the beginning of the church year. It begins on the fourth Sunday before Christmas and ends December 24.

NOVEMBER

flower mums

BIRTHSTONE
topaz
FOR FAITHFULNESS

To improve the soil, spread manure on plowed fields before the ground freezes and harrow it in. Farmers who live along the seashore should haul in sea wrack and plow it into the land.

With the weather turning cold, it will soon be time to do the slaughtering. Though you are looking forward to fresh spareribs, sausages, and hogshead cheese, the filling of the pork barrel should be the first order of business, for its contents must last until November of next year. Trim the pieces, pack them carefully, salt them, cover them with brine, and return the barrel to the cellar.

Turkeys do not thrive when confined to a pen and should be allowed to forage in the woods for fallen nuts (mast). The birds will find fewer crickets, grasshoppers, and other insects at this time of the year, so increase their other food—buckwheat, oats, barley, and corn. Feed them at night; they will roam in the morning but come home early and roost safely around the farm buildings.

After the garden is cleaned up, the weeds and rubbish burned to destroy seeds and harmful insects, how pleasant it is to consider the making of mince pies!

WEATHER WISE

- THE GOOSE BONE METHOD OF PREDICTING THE WEATHER:

When the fun and feasting's done,
  find the breastbone of the goose;
    pry it loose.
    Place it on the sill to dry.
    Keep your eye
on the color of the bone.
If the bone turns chalky white
you'll be snug and warm at night.
If the bone turns black or blue
winter will go hard on you.

- The number of days between the new moon and the first snowfall deep enough to track a cat will tell you how many snow-falls to expect during winter.

If on trees the leaves still hold,
The coming winter will be cold.

- **Winter apples** (November to March):

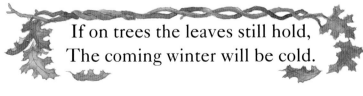

Baldwin · Rhode Island · Greening · Northern Spy

Tompkins King · Roxbury · Russet · Spitzenburg

NOVEMBER

WORTH KNOWING

In 1872 the bald eagle became the U.S. emblem. Earlier Benjamin Franklin had argued for the wild turkey: "The turkey is in comparison a much more respectable bird . . . a bird of courage."

The turkey is native only to America, unlike the eagle, which is found in many parts of the world.

THE BENEFITS OF SALT:

Warm saltwater used as a gargle or mouthwash is a good remedy for colds, sore throats, and sore gums.

When washing windows in winter, add salt to the water and the glass will not turn frosty.

Colored clothes will not run if you add salt to the water in which you wash them.

Joe Kinman, a pioneer settler near Fond du Lac, Wisconsin, had four horses to help him work his farm between the years 1849 and 1869. When they died, he buried them with a marker and an epitaph:

Here lies Tom and Bill They done their duty With a will

Also Doll and Kate As true and faithful As their mates.

Onions are helpful to those with coughs, colds, and influenza. Eating an onion every other day will help to clear your complexion.

To break up a cold, roast a lemon, fill it with sugar, and eat it hot before retiring.

WORTH COOKING

Mincemeat (about 10 quarts)

COMBINE:

- 4 lbs. lean chopped beef
- 2 lbs. chopped beef suet
- 1 peck peeled, cored, sliced Baldwin apples
- 3 lbs. sugar
- 2 quarts cider
- 4 lbs. seeded raisins
- 3 lbs. currants
- 1 1/2 lbs. chopped citron
- 1/2 lb. dried chopped orange peel
- 1/2 lb. dried chopped lemon peel
  juice and rind of 1 lemon
- 1 tbsp. each cinnamon, mace, and cloves
- 1 tsp. pepper
- 1 tsp. salt
- 2 whole grated nutmegs
- 1 gallon sour cherries with juice
- 2 lbs. broken nutmeats

Cook these ingredients slowly for 2 hours. Stir them frequently. Seal in jars.

THE VOICES

In bad weather, we got rides to school. On very cold days, the Model T wouldn't start, so my father would soak a rag in kerosene, get under the car, light the rag, and hold it under the oil pan to warm it up. I stood by and watched, worried only that I might be late for school.

—ALBERTA REIMER

THE VOICES

We made the casings for the sausages. The intestine has a lining on it, and you scrub that lining till it flakes off and then you turn the intestine inside out and scrub it again. And that casing is thin and white and clean as snow.
—ALTON WOLF

other was terribly afraid of the water. When the ice froze in low spots in the field, Mother would call out, "Don't fall through!"
—LORETTA KORFHAGE

f it hadn't been for your grandmother, my dad would have frozen to death. See, they walked home from St. John's School, four or five miles. The English River froze up solid, so they walked on the ice to get out of the wind. My dad wanted to lie down and go to sleep. Now, that's the last thing you should do in the cold. And your grandmother kept him a-going till she got him home.
—HAROLD WIEDOW

ell, I'd say the doctor came quite often. For pills and medicines, he gave us powders wrapped in paper. I never did get the mumps, but I did have the measles. My younger brother Clarence died when he was a little over a year. He choked to death of whooping cough. My father felt terrible that he had no picture of Clarence, so he had someone take a picture of him in the coffin.
—L. K.

In my dad's family three children died of diphtheria in a week. His mom wrapped them up and handed them out the window. The baby was still nursing, and she didn't get it. I don't know how come Dad never got it. The house was quarantined.
—A. W.

t funerals, after the minister performed the service, we all went to the grave and threw flowers into it, after the coffin was lowered.
—L. K.

ometimes we'd butcher a pig. My father would do it. I'd keep my ears shut. My mother would fry the meat and put it in a crock, and she'd let the fat run over the whole thing to keep it, so that maybe on a Sunday when we came home from church, she could dig up some of those pork chops from the crock.
—L. K.

WINTER

Barn on ALBERTA REIMER's farm, built when she was about eight or nine years old

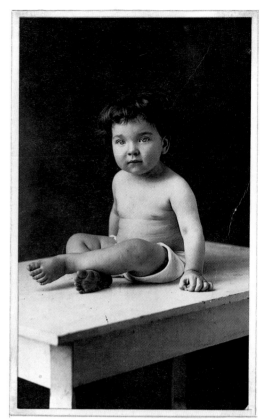

ALBERTA REIMER

LORETTA KORFHAGE *(left)* and sister, MILDRED

ALBERTA *(right)* with sister, DORA, and brother, HARRY

Top row (left): ALBERTA's grandfather's store

Top row (right): ALTON WOLF *(right)* and sister, HAZEL

Middle row (left): Interior view of W. W. JOHNSON store

Middle row (right): ALBERTA *(right)* with cousin, sister, and brother

Bottom: Barn built by GROSSVATER WIEDOW

"I," said the donkey, all shaggy and brown,
"I carried His mother uphill and down,
   I carried her safely to Bethlehem town."
"I," said the donkey, all shaggy and brown.

"I," said the cow, all white and red,
"I gave Him my manger for a bed,
   I gave Him my hay to pillow His head."
"I," said the cow, all white and red.

"I," said the sheep with the curly horn,
"I gave Him my wool for a blanket warm,
   He wore my coat on Christmas morn."
"I," said the sheep with the curly horn.

Twelfth-century English carol
THE FRIENDLY BEASTS

VARIABLE HOLIDAYS

HANUKKAH

The eight-day Festival of Lights honors the victory of the Jews over their enemies twenty-one hundred years ago. The victory allowed them to regain the temple in Jerusalem, and they were eager to rededicate the temple. Though they found only enough oil to last one day, the lamp burned for eight days. On each of the eight days of Hanukkah a candle is lit in the menorah to celebrate the miracle.

DATES AND FESTIVALS

6 *Day of St. Nicholas,* the fourth-century Bishop of Myra, patron saint of Russia. It is he, not Santa Claus, who brings gifts to children in Russia and many other parts of Europe.

7 *Willa Cather,* writer, is born, 1873.

10 *Emily Dickinson* is born, 1830.

12 *Fiesta of Our Lady of Guadalupe* The Virgin Mary appears to an Indian convert, Juan Diego, in 1531 and asks for a church to be built. To help Diego convince the bishop, she fills his blanket with roses and leaves her own portrait painted on it.

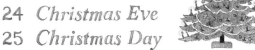

13 *Day of St. Lucia,* Queen of Light. In Sweden the girl chosen to be St. Lucia rises early and serves coffee and buns shaped like cats' heads to the members of her family.

16 The Boston Tea Party, 1773

21 *Winter solstice*

22 *Alton Wolf* is born, 1913.

23 *Sarah "Madam C. J." Walker,* a businesswoman who made hair products and was the first self-made millionaire in America, is born, 1867.

23 Colonists repeal the ban on Christmas festivities, 1681.

24 *Christmas Eve*

25 *Christmas Day*

26 through January 1. *Kwanzaa* (from the Swahili word meaning "first fruits"). A week when African Americans come together to celebrate their African heritage.

corn symbolizes CHILDREN

28 *Holy Innocents Day,* or *Childermas,* the day that honors the children killed by King Herod when he tried to destroy the infant Jesus. It is considered the unluckiest day of the year.

FARMER'S CALENDAR

flower ~ holly   BIRTHSTONE • *turquoise*
FOR WEALTH

Look over the notebook you've kept about how you managed your farm. Pay attention to any mistakes you may have made so that you can avoid repeating them.

With winter storms coming, ask yourself if there is a sick neighbor whose woodpile is running low. Good neighbors make good neighborhoods.

Your animals are now shut in their winter quarters. Rub down and blanket the horse that's wet or tired, and do not let your horses stand in the wind.

Cold weather is the time to slaughter hogs, for the meat will not spoil.

Reading is a fine way to pass the leisure hours of winter.

A slice of lemon or raw potato rubbed on your hands will help rid them of stains.

WORTH KNOWING

 Among reindeer and caribou, both males and females have antlers.

Reindeer Mary founded a large company that dealt in reindeer meat near Point Barrow, Alaska, at the turn of the century.

A traditional Christmas tree ornament from Germany is the glass pickle. The first child to find it receives an extra present from St. Nicholas.

"A Visit from St. Nicholas" by Clement C. Moore was first published anonymously in the *Troy Sentinel,* 1823.

DECEMBER

In Scandinavia farmers include birds and animals in the Christmas celebration. Traps, snares, and nets are removed so that even fish and wild creatures can enjoy the season. Cattle and horses receive an extra portion of oats or barley and the farmer's greeting: "It's Christmas Eve, good friend. Eat well."

Piñatas were first made, not in Mexico, but in Italy, in the fourteenth century. They were called "pignattas" and were shaped like ice cream cones. The word for the shape was "pigna"; hence their name.

COW FACTS

- A newborn calf weighs between 60 and 105 pounds at birth. A full-grown cow weighs about 1,400 pounds.

- An average cow in Wisconsin gives about 17,000 pounds of milk a year, or 2,125 gallons.

- One gallon of cow's milk weighs about eight pounds.

WEATHER WISE

When the needles on the pines turn to the west, look for snow.

If Christmas Day on Thursday be, A windy winter you shall see.

WORTH COOKING

Latkes (Grated Potato Pancakes)

6 medium potatoes
1 onion
2 eggs
1/2 cup flour
1 teaspoon salt
oil for deep frying

Pare potatoes and grate into a mixing bowl. Squeeze out liquid. Peel onion and grate into potatoes. Add eggs, flour, and salt, and stir to make a smooth batter that drops heavily from the spoon. Heat the oil in a heavy frying pan. Drop the batter from a spoon into the hot oil, making the pancakes three inches across. Fry over moderate heat until brown on both sides.

THE VOICES

Before Christmas my parents would take me to the toy store, and I would look and look and look, and then I could select just one thing that I wanted and I'd get that for Christmas. One year I got a little china cabinet. It had two doors with glass panes and two drawers underneath. I had two tea sets, but one was very special and I could only play with that once in a while. Another year I got a little stove.

We had a doll cradle and lots of dolls. I named mine Adeline. My sister's doll was named Cheruschia. There was a song we used to sing in school: "Cheruschia, put the kettle on, and we'll all take tea."

—LORETTA KORFHAGE

THE VOICES

e never wrapped our presents. We put out big plates for Christmas—we'd find the biggest plates in the china cupboard and our presents were put on these plates. Each child had a plate.

—ALBERTA REIMER

Mamma would send to Sears Roebuck and order something for Christmas. One year she sent away and got a five-pound box of hard candy. She hid it in the north room, and I found out where she hid it, and I'd sneak in there and eat it. Oh, did I get sick on that green candy.   —HAROLD WIEDOW

ur tree was a big limb my father cut from the cedar trees. We decorated it with paper ornaments and tinsel, balls, and candles in tin holders. We got new twisted candles each year. We put the tree in the dining room on a sewing machine base, since it was not as tall as a real tree.

We would light the candles on Christmas Eve. There was a green oilskin window shade that caught fire one year. I grabbed the doll I got for Christmas. My father told us all to go outside. It was dark, and I ran toward the south road. My father put the fire out, but the tree and the curtains burned.   —A. R.

e went to a Christmas Eve program at church. We always wore long black stockings. We had only one pair of shoes that either buttoned or buckled. It was always cold on the way to church, even though the car had side curtains. But the church was warm. There were two entrances. The men sat on one side, the women and children on the other. There was a room at the back of the church where women with babies sat.

It was a country church with no electric lights. There were kerosene fixtures on the wall and a huge Christmas tree with candles that were lit on Christmas Eve. The services were always in German.

After the program, the men passed paper bags out to the children filled with peanut brittle, candy, nuts, and an orange.   —A. R.

hen I was back in Kansas I went to see the tree I planted from a seedling one day as I played farm under the cedar trees.   —A. R.

ACKNOWLEDGMENTS

The author and illustrator wish to thank Robert Korfhage and Sharon McKay for sharing their family photographs.

And thanks to Charles Briggs, for sharing the story about St. Isidore, and to the State Historical Society of Wisconsin, whose excellent collection of books and exhibits was enormously useful.

The author gratefully acknowledges the following:

American Farm & Home Almanac 1994, by Ray Geiger. Almanac Publishing Company, 1994.

Country Gardener's Almanac, by Martin Lawrence. The Main Street Press, 1984.

Days and Customs of All Faiths, by Howard V. Harper. Fleet Publishing Company, 1957.

Jerry Baker's Fast, Easy Vegetable Garden, by Jerry Baker. Penguin Books, 1985.

First Americans 1994 Engagement Calendar, by Phil Bellfy and Judith Dupré. Random House, 1994.

Miscellany of Garden Wisdom, by Bernard Schofield. Running Press, 1990.

National Trust Calendar of Garden Lore, by Julia Jones and Barbara Deer. Dorling Kindersley, 1989.

Old Farmers Every Day Calendar 1994 Almanac, by Robert B. Thomas. Random House, 1994.

Royster's Almanac. F. S. Royster Guano Co., 1911.

The following poems and extracts are reproduced with permission:

Hopi Kachina Song for a Corn Planting Dance, p. 32, and "A Vision of Handsome Lake," p. 40, from *The Magic World: American Indian Songs and Poems*, selected and edited by William Brandon (Ohio University Press, 1991). Reprinted with permission of The Ohio University Press/Swallow Press, Athens.

"Boiling the sap to make maple syrup," p. 19, from *Chippewa Child Life and Its Cultural Background*, by M. Inez Hilger (St. Paul: Minnesota Historical Society Press, 1992). Reprinted with permission of The Minnesota Historical Society Press.

"The sun's feet . . .", p. 12, by Li Ho appeared in *Five T'Ang Poets*, Field Translation Series, v. 15, © 1991. Oberlin College Press: translated by David Young. Reprinted with permission of the Oberlin College Press.

Selections from poems by Emily Dickinson, pp. 18, 36, reprinted by permission of the publishers and the Trustees of Amherst College from *The Poems of Emily Dickinson*, Thomas H. Johnson, ed., Cambridge, Mass.: The Belknap Press of Harvard University Press, copyright © 1951, 1955, 1979, 1983 by the President and Fellows of Harvard College.

Quote from Nellie Kedzie Jones, p. 48, from *Advice to Farm Women: Letters from Wisconsin, 1912–1916*, ed. Jeanne Hunnicutt Delgado, vol. 57, no. 1, autumn 1973, p. 24. Reprinted with permission of the State Historical Society of Wisconsin.

Weather poems, pp. 24, 41, 55, 62, from *The Book of Weather Clues*, compiled by Diane Kaiser (Starrhill Press, 1986). Reprinted with permission of Starrhill Press.